Kevin Crossley - Holland's
EAST ANGLIAN POEMS

*First published
in a hand-printed edition
limited to 100
signed and numbered copies
December 1988
by James Dodds at
Jardine Press, Stoke by Nayland
Suffolk CO6 4SD, England*

*Details of Jardine Press editions
can be obtained from
this address*

Kevin Crossley - Holland's
EAST ANGLIAN POEMS

with illustrations by James Dodds

Jardine Press
1989

An Approach to the Marsh
The First Island
Spring Tide, Burnham-Overy-Staithe
Dusk, Burnham-Overy-Staithe
Shadows
The Wall
Confessional
Geese
The Signs of Walsham
Do You, or I, or Anyone Know?
A Walsham Harvest
Angels at St Mary's
A Tongue of Flint
Comfort
Eastern Light
Here, at the Tide's Turning

The poems in this collection
have been selected from
The Rain-Giver (1972)
The Dream-House (1976)
Time's Oriel (1983)
Waterslain (1986)
The Painting-Room (1988)
The first two volumes
were published
by Andre Deutsch
and the last three
by Century Hutchinson

Second edition 1989

© James Dodds 1988

© Kevin Crossley-Holland 1988

ISBN 0 9509270 7 4

I have never lived on the north Norfolk coast but it is and always has been my heartland. Actual and fantastic walk hand-in-hand in its stark theatre, its mesh of sand dune, shingle ridge, saltmarsh and creek, and each is as real as the other: the island of Scolt Head, an earthly paradise, can all too suddenly disappear; the great marsh is sometimes covered with licking blue flames; dark ribs sweep across it and, in the stillness of dusk, the noise-god follows them.

But I have followed the flight-paths of the wild geese far inland and settled in a pink Suffolk village: Walsham-le-Willows. How busy it is! And how ancient! Lapped by barley and shielded by sovereign trees, the place is instinct with its own history: hammerbeam roof, virgin's crant, grace-and-favour houses. It is not Eden but it is human.

So the seasons dance in a ring . . . The birds emigrate and I return to the harsh coast. Wind-blast and sea-slam! It is a secular confessional. The defining crystalline light creates its own illusions and paradoxes. And the marsh: what is constant about the marsh except for its state of flux? Years ago, as a boy, I took all this for granted; now, I do not. But for child and poet, this is the space where everything becomes possible.

Kevin Crossley-Holland

James Dodds is a painter whose ideas and whose work have been moulded by seascapes, the elements, and themes of timelessness. More specifically the Suffolk coast, ships, and nautical folklore form the basis from which many of his concepts derive. He has made splendid illustrations to Peter Grimes. In this sense he is an artist whose work has a strong regional setting. His imagery is terse but never bleak. In the words of one of George Crabbe's poems they enable us to see "the tides reflowing sign". In doing so his work becomes both moving and remarkably memorable.

Peter de Francia

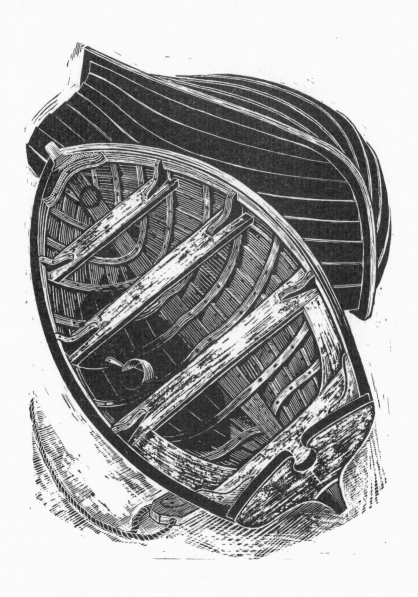

An Approach to the Marsh

The rope is almost paid out here. Bawdeswell
and the ghost of its foul reeve left to stew,
I drive down cool green naves, and soon the lanes
begin to ripple. More pilgrims are shuffled off
to the shrine at Walsingham, and that is an end
to the firm ground of conviction. This is no man's land
that never belongs to earth or sea entirely:
now the flowing barley hemmed by screaming poppies,
a gull perched on a salt-rusted ploughshare
and a gull, a litter of blood-tarred feathers,
festering. A veil of butterflies, opalescent,
dips and quivers and rises, and I come to where
there is no going beyond.
                              Marsh, mud, shifting sand,
creeks sinuous and shining, they look sucked
and rendered almost certain by the sun;
but now and then, and for no evident reason,
rigging yaps, or seabirds shriek at what we cannot
even see, or the sea broadcasts over the marsh. . . .
This bleached boat, that dabber, those children
gathering samphire, leaping over sun-crazed pulks:
the staithe today rests on its August oars;
hard light gives an edge to all that's apparent,
where nothing is what it seems or not for long.

The First Island

There it was, the island.

Low-slung sandhills like land-waves, fettered by marram.
One hut, a dark nugget. Across the creeks gleaming like
tin, like obsidian, across the marshes almost rust,
olive, serge, fawn, purpled for a season, the island.

We shoaled on the Staithe, stared out and possessed it;
children who collar half the world with a shout, and
share it in a secret.

Old men sat on a form lodged against the wall.
Of course we did not ask. We knew. They were too old.

There it was, and at times not there. Atmosphere
thickened, earth and air and water became one lung;
we were in a wilderness.

In a coat of changing colours it awaited us. In the
calm seas of our sleep it always loomed, always ahead.
We woke, instantly awake. As if we never had been
tired, and all things were possible.

So the boat came for us. The island stretched out to
us and we took it for granted. And no one asked by
which creeks we had come or could return.

Spring Tide, Burnham - Overy - Staithe

Sea undermines the sand-cliffs,
unties marram knots.

Surges of dark water
sweep sand into the creeks

patrolled by pirate skuas.
Shrikes and kittiwakes

fly in with the flood,
driven from their drift-nests

on Scolt Head. The groynes,
channels, side-gullies

cannot contain this tide;
white sea-stallions

race over the saltmarsh,
thrift and thistle and mud.

Waves lap, and slap
the base of Burnham dyke

that frowns, unforgetful
of the great flood. Gorse

half-hides its scars – sandbags
cement blocks, giant spars.

Bitterns boom their warning
now as the water rises.

Men shoal on the Staithe.

Dusk, Burnham - Overy - Staithe

The blue hour ends, this world
floats on a great stillness.

I only guess where marsh
finishes and sky begins,

each grows out of the other.
In the creek a slip

of water gleams. Rowboats
bob and swing above the mud,

the barnacled and broken
ribs of Old Stoker's boat.

A wedge of gulls rustles
overhead, and for a moment

the water notices them.
Such calm is some prelude.

Then across the marsh it comes,
the sound as of an endless

train in a distant cutting,
the god working his way back,

butting and shunting,
reclaiming his territory.

This world's his soundbox now;
in the stillness he still moves.

Anything could happen.

Shadows

A rib of shadow on the marsh,
It grows like a dark thought;

My skull begins to gather
All the far-off booming of the sea.

A crab's skeleton disintegrates
Between my careful fingers

And the salt harvest where I stand
Gleams like guttering candle-ends.

O most loved when almost lost,
This most uncommon common place,

Still at dusk mysterious,
My sea-threatened wilderness . . .

The dark wave sweeps through me.
A rib of shadow on the marsh.

The Wall

I am a desolate wall, accumulator of lichen.
Men made me with flint chippings and, fickle as always,
ignored me; time did not ignore them.
My business is to divide things: the green ribbons
of grass from the streams of macadam; the kitchen gardens
from the marsh acres, garish with sea-lavender;
the copses of ilex and pine from the North Sea,
the bludgeoning waves of salt water where seabirds play.
I stand grey under the East Anglian sky,
glint when the occasional sun opens its eye.

My business is to divide things, my duty to protect.
I am unrepaired; men neglect me at their own risk.
Time takes me in mouthfuls; the teeth of the frost
bit into my body here; here my mortar crumbles;
the wind rubs salt into every wound.
Elsewhere I am overgrown with insidious ivy;
it wound its arms around me only to strangle me.

Relentless, the sea rolls down from the Pole.
It levelled the dunes last year, removed the marram grass,
clashed its steel cymbals over marsh and macadam.
It attacked me and undermined me; I sway
like a drunkard now; yet it could not gash me
with its gleaming scythes; it was not strong enough.
I stand, sad, and stare at all this estate,
the lawns, the kitchen gardens, copses garrulous
in the wind. I carefully listen, listen and wait
for the fierce outsider to force his way in.

Confessional

I come once more to this terrible place;
As it was it is, each stone and each face

Unchanged, making an index of the change
In me. Everything here was arranged

Long ago; the wind, raking from the north,
Saw to that and sees to it. In the hearth

Coals glow and the ash flies early and late;
Every face is ruckled, sands corrugate;

Inland, those superstitious hawthorn trees
Strain away from the wind and heckled seas.

Yet I come. Here alone I cannot sham.
The place insists that I know who I am.

Elemental trinity – earth, air, sea –
Harshly advocate my humility:

You are bigoted, over-ambitious,
You are proud, you salute the meretricious.

Then I have altered this much with the years:
That I need more to admit my errors,

From fear, and a longing not to be blind;
So I am scoured by the unchanging wind,

And rid again of some superfluity
By that force uninterested in me.

And I can go, prepared for the possible;
Dream and bone set out from the confessional.

Geese

At the skim of evening
Wild geese fly inland

Then immense silence
Sends most men to their houses

The Signs of Walsham

I have seen the way in. Right angles and rubber swerves
and deep scummy ditches. I have seen the puzzle on the
palimpsest: the forest of elm and ash, the watering
places.

I have seen the green women, all very elegant and very
particular, trilling in forever light painted in tempera.

I have seen matriarchs who buried their husbands. The
rectitude of pit-props; last survivors. Dispensers of
pullets' eggs and grace-and-favour houses.

Also the old snorters, beady, broad and blunt. I have
seen their terrible horizons.

A woman drifted she died while spring whistled at her
window. A newborn baby lolled in the shadow of the yew
tree. I have seen them.

I have seen tides: exiles from collapses and sagging
thatches, shoals of children, the lissom baby-sitters.
Also the old soaks, looking meaningful; buzzing week-
enders; nasal upstarts aspiring to jacuzzis.

I have seen the crusader who lost his name his date and
the crant for poor Mary who lost her heart and died. I
have seen the tradesmen hiding in the wall, the leftover
smiles of oak angels.

I have seen lists of sponsors and meringue-makers, paragraphs of small type concerning covenants.

Every eighth minute the Bangalore Bomber. The light plane stoops with its deadly spray. The F1-11s set out for Libya. I have seen them.

I have seen the kestrel and the tree-creeper; the sun-splash butterflies; the blue sheen on a dragonfly's wings.

The circle of smiles ringing the pink cottages; I have seen it. I have seen slight shoulders, stooping shoulders sharing heavy weather.

Change-ringers stand in the tower. Clay throws up gold. I have seen layer upon layer. And every day this jack-wind and its small rearrangements.

Do You, or I, or Anyone Know ?

It comes up by the roots
                         dangling and unfortunate,
a straggler and victim on the field's margin
never quite caught up in the bruised gold tides.

The air's an intoxicant, laced with the sweetness
of the barley, and clay, and far thunder.

You shake off the chaplet of storm-flies
and, sharp as a bright stoat, bite through
the hempen stalk.
                   You're holding a wand.

A lick of lightning...
                      You break off one grain
and tickle it round the cradle of your palm.
It's a kingdom! First you peel away
pale-striped bullseye skin, then plain wrapping.

And now, half-a-minute later, the dark sky-growl.
The storm's still half-a-county off!
                           The smiling cleft;
the ivory sheen; the warm grain still malleable.

You grind it and grit it. Unconvinced
of its relationship to barley-water, you spit it out.

Now the beard: one whisker. You hold the hilt
and run it smoothly between your fingers.
You rub it the wrong way and say 'It's biting!'

Nothing the eye can see,
                              unlike the storm
gathering and sending shivers through the barley,
but simply a feeling:
                              leading to this good sense
that things are seldom what they seem
and questions teem with other questions.

Later, you lift my little brass microscope
from its wooden box.
                              How you surprise my childhood!
Properly ginger, you lay the whisker on the glass tray.

I light the kitchen candle – rain-spears and thunder
drive in through the garden gate –
and fiddle with the mirror, the tube, the mirror...

Barba dentata: covering one eye with soft fingertips
you level your unblinking gaze.

A Walsham Harvest

The sky: violet and then
and only then
in this right-angled honest place
so intense it quivered.
It broke the rules.

Fire's glottals
hacked through hedge and thicket,
its pale scarves trussed
the bullace the lichenous crab apple;
crack cracked the willow.

So the moon loped
up, quickened
in the breathing spaces,
over the blond corn
this lopped thing, this ladle of blood.

Foggy and very close, one blast
to begin
this evening of long intervals.
Cough; creak; creak; scuffle.
All ears and stoops.

Angels at St Mary's

'The angels have gone.'
Church Guide, Walsham-le-Willows

Up among bleached stars and suns
Are the tongues, protruding, oak pegs
Wanting their smiling high-fliers.

The fledglings heard black hints
And saw battle-lights advancing.
They conferred, they spread their wings.

Or did they become spirits of
Themselves? Angels rearranged,
Acute angles where clear sound and

Sunlight cross? They are in the air.

A Tongue of Flint

I kicked it out of its snug in a mole-hill,
flecked and milky,
               and listen to it sing
far from home
          how in those same and everyday
acres with their may-hedges and hedges
jewelled with hips, and all those generations
of seething mosquitoes under the oaks,

I sat on the stile
                or stood by the almost
stagnant stream to watch the swift year's wavings.

No breath of wind,
                    nothing but burning cold,
and one old oak dropped half its leaves.
They shaved from limb to limb: a sound near
the edge of sound – the sharpest scraping.

High summer, setting sun. Ten silhouettes,
hefty and black, whisked filthy tails.
                                They spun,
they wove rose wheels and golden fans.

Then I heard them
                feverish and shrill
and saw the elm quiver. A siege of starlings
singing well above themselves! Two thousand
or ten thousand footnotes and tripping glosses
or the colours of the year.
                        Up, then, up and off
against banks of pearl and grey, shape-changers,
raucous spirits . . .
                    This tongue, fierce light
has knapped it and east wind stropped it.
I'll pocket it
            and go on listening.

Comfort

Who said anything about comfort?
Those syllables do not rhyme
with zinc slakes or ice-bright sky.
The sea is grinding her spears.
Up creeks and gullies, over groynes
the black tide surges
and the hag wind rides her.
In the black forest on the staithe
rigging clacks and chitters.

Little but memory for company,
wild geese, swans whooping,
but no urbanity no
gossip prejudice bitterness sham.
In London I dream of these harsh folds,
the sea's slam, the light's eagle eye,
and here again I draw
this place – hair shirt, dear cloak –
around such infirmities.

Eastern Light

for Jonathan Crossley-Holland

There was a time
when so little seemed uncertain.
I lounged beneath the green seigneurs
and viewed the huge sky stooping:
rinsed, I wrote, and *ringing,*
and *fluent,* and *lapidary.*

The light was a bright statement,
candid and clean as a Commandment,
a sword-stroke
admitting no half-measure.
Doubt itself seemed a sin.

In this indeterminate and empty
quarter, this mesh
of sanding and marsh and creek,
I see this is creation light;
unblinking light, severe and immense.
Does that mean it is true?

That boy climbing the dune's escarpment,
scrambling to the top of far Gun Hill
comes so close
we could call out to him.

In this frame
almost innocent of dampness
and bruises and concealment,
the tricks-in-trade of the misty west,
is there one blade,
one fault, one silver serpent,
you think you cannot clearly see?

You see what you think then?
Where is the deceit in equity?
Look east. Light of light.
I go back to the beginning.
Apparent, I write.

Here, at the Tide's Turning

You close your eyes and see
                                        the stillness of
the mullet-nibbled arteries, samphire
on the mudflats almost underwater,
and on the saltmarsh whiskers of couch-grass
twitching, waders roosting, sea-lavender
faded to ashes.

            In the dark or almost dark
shapes sit on the staithe muttering of plickplack,
and greenshanks, and zos beds;
                                        a duck arrives
in a flap, late for a small pond party.

The small yard's creak and groan and lazy rap,
muffled water music.

                         One sky-streamer,
pale and half-frayed, still dreaming of colour.

Water and earth and air quite integral:
all Waterslain one sombre aquarelle.

From the beginning, and last year, this year,
you can think of no year when you have
not sat on this stub of a salt-eaten stanchion.

Dumbfounded by such tracts of marsh and sky –
the void swirled round you and pressed against you –
you've found a mercy in small stones.

This year, next year, you cannot think
of not returning: not to perch in the blue
hour on this blunt jetty, not to wait, as of right,
for the iron hour and the turning of the tide.

You cross the shillying and the shallows
and, stepping on to the marsh, enter
a wilderness.

        Quick wind works around you.

You are engulfed in a wave of blue flames.

No line that is not clear cut and severe,
nothing Baroque or bogus. The voices
of young children rehearsing on the staithe
are lifted from another time.

                This is
battleground. Dark tide fills the winking pulks,
floods the mud-canyons.

            This flux, this anchorage.

Here you watch, you write, you tell the tides.

            You walk clean into the possible.